I0151345

Here, We Bury the Hearts

poems by

Dom Fonce

Finishing Line Press
Georgetown, Kentucky

Here, We Bury the Hearts

ACKNOWLEDGMENTS

Grateful acknowledgement to the following journals which these poems first
appeared:

3Elements Literary Review: "Neuroplasticity"
Black Rabbit Quarterly: "The Rain and the Rust"
Blacklist Journal: "The Elephant Man Visits Youngstown through a Portal from My
Eyes"
Bridge: The Bluffton University Literary Journal: "Standing over the Great Serpent
Mound, 2017"
Burning House Press: "Ghost Feet, Some Booze, and My Living Room: A Sad Party"
COG Magazine: "Falling asleep awake," "The Elephant Man's face is turned into a
Halloween mask, and I buy one"
Fourth and Sycamore: "Placement"
The GNU Journal: "Of Two Caverns"
Great Lakes Review: "An Elegy for the Lost Athens Sixty-two"
Italian Americana: "My Mother's Hair"
Jenny Magazine: "Portrait of Rock 'N' Roll as Car Crash"
Meow Meow Pow Pow Lit: "Portrait of Mr. Peanut as the Body Politic"
Mistake House Magazine: "The Sounds of Ash"
Ohio's Best Emerging Poets: An Anthology: "Flung"
Obra/Artifact: "Here, We Bury the Hearts"
Strata Magazine: "Undoings"
Tilde: "Ungrateful Dead"
The Tishman Review: "The air around us is a blanket"
UReCA: "Portrait of Youngstown as the Archetypal Fallen Kingdom"

Publisher: Leah Maines
Editor: Christen Kincaid
Cover Art: Dom Fonce
Author Photo: Joelle Lambert
Cover Design: Elizabeth Maines McCleavy

Printed in the USA on acid-free paper.
Order online: www.finishinglinepress.com
            also available on amazon.com

Author inquiries and mail orders:
Finishing Line Press
P. O. Box 1626
Georgetown, Kentucky 40324
U. S. A.

Table of Contents

For my mother and sister

Here, We Bury the Hearts

Any cemetery
left to its own devices
has no choice but to latch onto your chest
and snatch out
of you both existence and expiration.
Especially here.

In Cleveland,
the Rockefellers' grave touches
the sun. They lie there both very rich
and very dead.

Within my living room lay the
charred corpse of a great man.

It doesn't matter.
We bury the hearts first.

All of us.

It doesn't matter.

We've grown cocoons
and hear the pitter-patter of rain, of sleet—
the over-glaze of freeze—here are our trophies.
We must shield our chests.
Within our shoeboxes,
our coffins,
our mausoleums underneath
monuments,
you, an outsider, can hear a small thump,
a dun-dun in the distance, symphonically mount
as the dead rise to click rocks
and tap sticks to a single beat,
dun-dun,
dun-dun,
dun-dun—
to make music,
to dance.
And the country moves with us
as we drive out our red rivers.

Ungrateful Dead

> *My body I give to my dear friend Doctor Southwood Smith to be*
> *disposed of in a manner hereinafter mentioned…The skeleton he will*
> *cause to be put together in such a manner as that the whole figure may*
> *be seated in a chair usually occupied by me when living, in the attitude*
> *in which I am sitting when engaged in thought in the course of time*
> *employed in writing.*
> —from Jeremy Bentham's will

I.
When I die
fasten me up straight,
jam a lightbulb in my brain,
and crown me with a lampshade.

II.
"Eugene: Found Dead 1929, Buried 1964" is etched into his stone—
he is more famous than Elvis in these hinterland parts of Ohio,

a mummified porcelain doll, a beautiful drowned man on a beach
    of backroad—
washed onto gravel in beating-down sun. The townsfolk fashion cattail
    bracelets

for his shrunken wrists like they've found God. They put him on
    shoulders and
carry him up a mountain. Danse macabre, necrojubilee. Ghosts
    from beyond shake

and rattle to rhythmic music—some may wish to stay. All things must
    tarnish.
I wonder if concave, vacant eyeholes still rolled endlessly in Eugene's
    skull as

blood-filled hands moved his dehydrated frame from shopfront to
porch seat—the greatest Halloween decoration. Or maybe the gawker
spotlight curled up his long-crumbled

lip; perhaps his grey skin blushed—the ungrateful dead. Now, I let
    flowers settle on his stone
and long to lay them at his undead feet as if he were a cherished king—
    his face is an ancient,

haunted house that scares us as children and that we weep for
    in adulthood
as the city rules its demolition. If death hadn't snatched him again, into
    his

six-foot void, where no eyes could marvel his eccentricity, I could hold
    his bramble
hand in mine; I could pretend his spectacle was what he wanted.

III.
Images of a my beloved embalmed, statuesquely posing, a piece
of machinery pistoning her arm to wave at the passersby
of some Tri-State thrift shop—camera flash to inhale her
newfound life—made me partly grimace, partly warm up
in the chest.

For Amelia Conceller

In the envelope, next to a picture
of you, I found a card.

On May 24th, 1963, your services
were held at St. Theresa's Church
at 9:30 a.m., and you were to be buried
in Calvary Cemetery.

On May 8th, 1963,
you sent a letter to my great
grandmother in Leavittsburg
from Cleveland.

And on May 20th, you died.

In your letter, you were hopeful:
"My dear Nancy. It's grand
to have spring back again. The robins
here get you up in the morning."

You were a loving mother:
"I still have not found a job yet. Looks
like my children will not get very much
of my money to spent on themselfs
if I don't get work soon."

You were figuring your life out:
"My eyes are very bad, I am
not able to see much from my left eye.
After a few hours on my feet they swell
up very much. But I am going to try and work."

You were so lonesome:
"When I call any of my relatives
they tell me to come and see them
sometime. That sometime business
might be that they don't give a darn
about seeing me at all."

 And you felt so powerless:
"The trouble with me
is that I don't have much to say."

You were a person, like me.

This poem is for you, poor, sweet mother,
taken too soon.

Dun-dun-dun.

Do you hear your heart pounding on the page—
an ethereal reminder that you are not forgotten?

Portrait of Youngstown as the Archetypal Fallen Kingdom

In this scene, a cemetery, big as three towns, must sit
in the middle of the canvas. A splintered tree

must be nearing its fall, and a boy must walk past it
daily to see if it still stands tall. Only God knows

that its trunk will never snap to kindling shards
for the boy to make his fire with. The boy must be

a skeleton, and ghosts must twinkle in the foreground,
thin as newsprint, a bundle of spine balancing on pelvis.

A building is placed off to the side, just a slip
away from transforming into a scattershot pile

of rust. That is where the boy must rest every bruised
night. And there is me, a black cloud swirling by, looking

down at those of decay, knowing that the smell
of gold had once filled the air, feathering the world.

The Elephant Man Visits Youngstown through a Portal from My Eyes

His plan to spread the possibilities of life out in front of him is now spoiled in my stare. He sees the gum-stuck rust in my smile, himself in the bumping Oakhill beauty-marks that line the effigied earth. His ultimate notion: get me out of this man's range. Immured in brainy bulwarks, tranced in cross over, he's gone into a used-to-be home where a tree grows from the basement to the roof. Here, Merrick meets his match—something truly ugly to the world—a wendigo, welding-patched, red-eyed, nearly robotic, standing across the way, coursing sparks from his mouth. The Elephant Man's face turns and tills and tries to escape the structure's agonies. Seeing his disgust, the beast calls out in electric flicker, "I am a human being." The words crack Merrick's mind, and though they only hang an air of nebulous importance in his psyche—the way a dumb boy comprehends why a pretty girl flips her hair—the vowel and consonant soup tastes good off his lips. Within, he now knows he will end up dying young like me, that tiny towns kill those big thoughts of snatching a way out. Without, he rubs his eyes, scraping away my unwanted image.

Of Two Caverns

> *The frame of the cave leads to the frame of man.*
> —Stephen Gardiner

With a drip-

                    drip-

drip,

calcite fingers nearly join in tacking
embrace—tap and twist to turn ceiling
to floor—in two Ohio caverns.

One rusts and smuts from human
thumbprints and crumbles under the weight
of urban sprawl in Youngstown.
A factory with blown-away—no, blasted-
out—war-wrecked window panes of a lost
economic kingdom.

Another is shaved from earth, carves
an opening to Nature's
carnivorous mouth that echoes, "Come on in.
No need to worry."
There, in that other town, the Heart-State
fae rubberneck corners
and flutter from pearly tooth to milky canine,
hiding their frail secrets
from the fee-payers. Behind backs, you can hear
their hand-cupped snickering as they
glee from crack to crevice.

Back in Youngstown, a vagrant and brambling
steel—a welding-fused wendigo—share
beans over a blazing fire on the fourth floor, peer
through those battle-torn panes, see abandon
like crashed airplanes hilling down
horizon lines.

The two look up, split a glance, catching
the cacophonous drumming of drip-drip-drip.

The same sound you hear
between the tour guide's droning
speech—as polaroid flash steals
your peripheral—and the cackles of cavern-sprites
in that other Ohio town.

Portrait of Rock 'N' Roll as Car Crash

At first, and with little knowledge of life's workings,
we twirled ourselves down hillsides just to see
the sky from the perspective of grass and the spin
of rolly-pollies from the eyes of clouds.

Then we found love in purple lipstick
and the glimpse of a little skin—tangled
together under bedsheets like strands of DNA.

Then we threw rocks at cars in a mist
of the Dead Kennedys and weed smoke,
wanting desperately to turn the world red.

Finally, we threw ourselves off cliffs in cars
that rattled like rat cages. We did so to knock back the choke
of rust and regret. We did so because we sucked
in more being than we could hold.

The Rain and the Rust

Everywhere the chew of pipes branching / through copper soil
could be heard. —Rochelle Hurt, "In the Century of Lunch Pails"

I hear the patter past
the pipes above; the roof
plays craps with itself.
In Youngstown, crystal spheres lick
leafy blades and levitate
zenith like earth-crust
into core and back out
through pore—a welding-fused
wendigo, once silver, is now brown
and planted, a statue, in the center of a
downtown street. Those who brave
the storm and sit in their cars must
honk horns at this poor beast, who
croaks through a mouth spliced
shut by drizzle turned lava.
Like it, the wet too makes us stone
and stuck within
our broken bar-lit
reflections inside busted bathroom
mirrors. Some things never change:
the bulbs flicker on and off
like the moon
does as its batteries begin to die—
you must shake it, smack it, send it
back to bright. The locks never turn,
the paper towels are
unsurprisingly missing, and
droplets forever steal the sky,
oxidize and decay our town
like atrophy in each and every
breathing body cell.

Neuroplasticity

The tragedy of growing old is not that one is old, but that
one is young.   —Oscar Wilde, *The Picture of Dorian Gray*

It's malleability and rigidity
                    that petrifies my brain of itself.

It crawls and claws between temple,
                    from picto-stimulants of nose-blowing

or dog-sniffing—those
                    everyday observations that

rabbit-hole to rhinorrhea research
and look-ups of chemoreception.   But Einstein was a genius at
    fifteen, right?

                    Such solidity at twenty-three;
    such churning goo at twenty-two.

                    When will we know when it all turns and
stops?
        Visitation to Princeton, Yale, and mental yard sale

                    to pick and purchase all these little thoughts.
    What if I'm thinking nasty things when it all stones?

                    Thinking about the thinking when I can't think as well
                    as I can think now.
I hear the whisper:
When will it all rock?
When will it all rock?

The Elephant Man's face is turned into a Halloween mask, and I buy one

off the Big Lots rack: plasticine clay, liquid latex, thickening gunk, paint that won't smudge away—that new mug smell. It suits me as I look at myself in the mirror. I rub the faux-boils, the drooping eye, try to talk a groan, become the freak show. And soon I feel a tug on my own cheeks through the continuum—fingers ridged and leathered running down every line of my face, tracing my nose, the centimetered difference between my eyes, the width of my mouth—a man in another dimension fitting me, modeling me, digging into my flesh like putty. Here, I learn what the corn kernel feels in the kettle—esophageal blasting heat waves crawl a reddening shriek, a pre-popped pod ready to burst, a mutating cell, an image being manipulated in time. I succumb to the touch, a fair trade, thinking this must've been what Leila felt when she and Joseph momentarily locked hands: Merrick hoping their connecting skin would conjoin two worlds, and Ms. Maturin faking to the universe that her love was bountiful enough for such a forbidding veil, just wanting to peek at mutilated wonder, to peer through the eyes of Hell alive.

Falling asleep awake

can never be like daydreaming. There, where space allows our futures to appear upon a platter, where the mind is less caged and freer to hop the field. No, falling asleep awake is for the ghosts—the specters of certainty and perhaps, the transitional mess between life and death. In half lucidity, my father stands behind me holding onto my shoulder, where you would be if you weren't in front of me now, and where red smells like birds chirping right outside my thunder-clomping window. Can you hear me? Do you understand that falling asleep awake is for the children when their parents have dozed off, thinking they've died? Like rugose limb rigor mortis, that entrapment of eyes within sockets, and brain stationed straight facing sinful film? No, it's not daydreaming. There's much too much wander in that fantasy. Here is where I shake your hand and don't but feel it and see it drop beneath me like liquid.

The air around us is a blanket

or
basalt prickling; the air is anything
but air.
And the science says it weighs
one-hundred pounds in any given walled-in space,
so is this tonnage on our napes, that presses onto

us like minnow does dock and
bone stock did marrow,
only the omnipresent,
inescapable huff-and-puffing
clearness of air?
Perhaps we should hold
our breath so not to overstrain our lungs
and bite our tongues and drain our brains of its massy grayish slop
and drop underground without the good clear
stuff like recovery, like addiction shakes
to see if it's the problem.

Or we can recapture it, weaponize it, solve it
like old words and blast through the world
to unmapped, wooded islands where the air is sweetest—
use it as a solvent and chug it down;
Where we go doesn't matter to me.
Or not, but the weight will keep on
weighing and the air will hang about incessantly,
either mockingly or in complete innocence: a problem or a solution.

Vision of the Elephant Man as a Graveyard

How many souls can your corpulent hands hold? My mother held two: mine and her own. I've carried stories of the long-gone and shared them, for better or worse, with the world, including your visions, Joseph. How many plotlines lie inside your transformed frame? Your skin gathers up in the way fabric folds, the way taffy tongues and turns. How much dead weight dragged the meat from your bones like teeth to a chicken wing? Enough for me to keep you alive—to place gravestones on your body and drudge along the cracked cemetery roads, looking for my father or grandfather who, in the end, both sagged under life's load just like you. Here, within you, is where all good men go—men who burden their curling backs with purpose, who shoulder their curse. No, Ephialtes won't be making an appearance on your hills, inside your tombs—that is not you. You are Hephaestus clang-clang-clanging in the ether, bang-banging your good work, though nobody sees it. No. I will not forget you, Joseph: keeper of good dead men who never complained.

My Mother's Hair

I have inherited the past turned crystal
 and cold. It disarranges in shapes that shuffle from
  my thumbnail, thick with excess. I see faces
 that have never mouthed my name but smile
  at me—shine at the world forever like they're
   wax dolls. I see my mother there, shocked
awake
  by flash-flicker, cemented into silence, forgotten
on film. Here, she's staked into timelines that
   she's veered away from and left behind,
  gifted to a different woman with
 different hair that hangs from her like a babushka ghosting
    through the air. Now she dyes
  away the silver like crying does to bad memories—a
stream veined through soil,
  tarnished by the dusty grains. My hair is like hers, long
 and unreasonable for a man—you will never catch me
   in front of a camera. Afraid to
  see myself years later—my head tackled
 and grated down to fuzz—and my lost expression, my
grasping for identity through the pores of my scalp. Each string that
 sheds
   to the ground I gather and rope into one
 and throw out to the past, to you, woman that's not
   my mother, that didn't understand
she would birth me, that never knew she could hurt the ones she
 loved
    in one gulp.
     Let me hoist you into
  the present and tell you of the future, your fortune,
  the hair you wear now, and all the things you
wish you wouldn't do but will, because each haircut is a symbol
   of a cut stabbed deep but survived—
  and, for you, there's a lot of life to live, and a lot of flesh
  to prick, and an infinite catalog of styles to choose from.

Undoings

I am out with lanterns, looking for myself.
—Emily Dickinson, in letter to J. G. Holland

After he died, my mother asked him, as the tears washed
into her bedsheets, if he would haunt her—"Please," she

said. "Please come back and touch me with your specter
hand." And she eventually stopped. "It didn't work," she said.

"There's no one left to listen." In some cosmic mishap, within
that tarry puddle where gone souls stay, he did hear, he did come

back, only not to her. At night, my ears ring with the cacophonous
soup of a single, wretched word: "Go!" When a father dies, a son dies
     too—

decisions, indecisions, changes, undoings. At the funeral, everyone
     told
me I was to take care of the world from then on, to dig out a path with
     a shovel

passed down from generation to generation. My father moves my
     hand.
His feet are my feet. Understanding is found underneath rocks the size

of doorways—gates of the pulseless. I budge no step without his
     ushering.
In the night, I howl at the moon and dig up graves with my back paws
     looking

for treasured manhood made physical and stately. My teeth sink into
     the gold piece.
I taste blood and lead—it pools in my mouth like soft gutter-water. I
     swordfight

trees and tie my tie around my waist. I wear my hat indoors and walk
     with my chest
small and hidden within itself. Sin fills my gut as I pray to him at
     church—

I pray the Lord lift the tension and leave me be—be with my mother, your wife,
who caws for you at midnight. I'll gnaw my thumbs to nubs just to see a doorknob

slip through my grasps; you'll place my hand on opportunity and it will fall to the ground
like a sheared head wheeling the lip of a bucket. The ether will echo your furious growl.

I'll wipe my brow and exhale. You'll be Zeus throwing bolts. I'll hide below the
stairwell and stash my ears in my back pockets and learn how to live in the dark without you.

Ghost Feet, Some Booze, and My Living Room: A Sad Party

the lawn / Is pressed by unseen feet, and ghosts return /
Gently at twilight, gently go at dawn. —T.S. Eliot, "To Walter de la Mare"

My father died in our living room.
                    The irony.

***

Every time the AC kicks on,
that damn dog barks at the
electrical click. Makes me want
to strangle him. When I was small,
I sat in front of the vents, blanketed
myself in the chill, and wondered if
Freon cannisters held ectoplasmic mist—
in my mind I saw logic in this business model,
carried a P.K.E. meter in one hand and
the future I hoped to have in the other.

***

I told my mother I was sure I'd seen a ghost.
                She told me, "Fuck off!
                        We all have our problems to deal with."
                    My father said
                            nothing; he wasn't even there.
My voice liquified; I'd gone away with him.

                        And the world swirled us down
                                into a   toilet bowl.
            ***

The retinas in my face
nuke the neurons through the cave
on my shoulders, crawl down
my throat and out my bladder until
I'm turned stone. I'm stuck cold.

I have no pulse. I'm zombic and
glassed-over, hearing the echo
of frost-breath swirling through
the air—the ghosts behind my eyes
leaking out.

***

A wish for mother (let the ghosts that leech on to your chest free):

Her vanity filled with doubloons—plastic
purples, reflective reds, swigless cyans—each
month to materially hold like Zen garden pebbles
that we scoop and let sift through the cracks of our
palms—in the way one peek-a-boos a child. Carry on now.
Stack stones like rolls of Standing Liberty coins.
Hang triangles around your wrists—close one eye
to focus forward past the jovial faces and those
itching urges you've battled and beaten throughout
Time's bursting waves.

***

In conversation with my mother and sister
              (the living room is bruised midnight-black
                        and cracks a laugh at us—
                  we hold dancing candles and huddle together
                          in our collective oranged sweat):
          "I think this house is alive. I think it wants us dead."

***

The neighbors notice
a blackhole eating
the house with one big bite, a statue
of me being shredded inside it.

***

The exorcism:

I shudder in bed. Everything
purrs. The salt of my forehead
rides the body zigzag as firing synapses
grunt in my legs. I'm a sack filled with
liquor and attitude. A finger makes
love to my throat. I must be half
alive, half in lust. A globe of glass
surrounds me—your face is bulbous
and infernal, yet you proceed. The house
jumps up and down from its cornerstones.
The windows awaken like fire and fall
like shuteye. Bang. Bang. Bang. In time,
and with much effort, you hook the
monster in my belly and slump its
body to the floor, soft as a newborn deer.

**Love Poem with an Eight-Thousand-Dollar House
on Cohasset Drive**

My love is a decrepit mansion found in the most forgotten back-road, Youngstown turn—flanked by roaming urban turkeys that cross the yard in formation like warriors underneath a mountain. It is being eaten by the woods—fetid to the marrow—with frame torn and tattered, the wilderness leaking inside like emptiness into a deer carcass. Yet it is alive with the faint mist of memories floating from its core through the blasted-in roof, in the way a crypt leaks ghosts from its cracks on a plum-skin night. My love is a future within those discolored bricks—a threaded robe of moth wings, bearded, waiting to lift, fluttering at once, wooshing away decade-plated dust. My love is the absorption found within the water-damaged walls, as pungent as the ringworm-spread of grief through a family. My love is a fever for shapes, of cloud-pricking peaks and cockeyed archway brows. I want this problem—fixing and healing, raw-rubbed hands—to be what I carry, a scar across my face, for the love of the city, art for art's sake. I want it, and its failing cornerstones, its fumbling bones, to nurture like a noisome garden, to become the castle and casket of my choosing.

An Elegy for the Lost Athens Sixty-two

Margaret Schilling,
　　　unforgettable in her febrile-filled lunacy,
　　　　　　　stained the attic floor with her roiled flesh
　　　　　and her name into the conscio-sphere forever.
But who are you, Athens Sixty-two?
　　　I hear the masturbatory shim-shimmying
　　　　　　　　　from every sweaty bunk
　　　　　throughout the halls, and
　　　　the crack-blasts
of phantom Union muzzleloaders in the war-fields, the electro-
　　　　　　　shock choke of remediation, and see
　　　　the insanity in their eyes.
But do I sense you, unnamed one
　　　　　　through sixty-two?
　　　Now we dig, lay our ears
　　to the grass
in search for your lonely heartbeats—
　　　you, your mysteries and misfortunes,
　　　understandable misgivings about us, are the adventures
for our future youths:
　　　　　　dun-dun, dun-dun, dun-dun.
　　　　　　　　　Can you hear it, Sixty-two?
　　　　　Your hearts thudding on the page
　　　　like a thousand medicinal, madhouse gulps:
　dun-dun, dun-dun, dun-dun.
　　　　　　Can you hear it?

Portrait of Mr. Peanut as the Body Politic

There's a bridge
in Youngstown
as magma-bright

as Mars dirt

and spindly-arched
as spider legs

caught and caged

a giant crab daggering
pincers into the Mahoning
over the horizon

stuck by rain-water oxidation
in the soot and muck

If you pass underneath

going downtown
you'll see him there
on the first I-beam

Him
there

Mr. Peanut

posing
cane in hand

Nobody knows why
yet we feel why

like wrapping
glittery tinsel
on a spruce
in the winter

a relic
a secret image binding us
into one spirit

of the city
the gluey weld

of each rustcd-out
rod

the bridge growls
cracks with the soul
of the people

each heart
and pump of life
now a clicking spinal disc

trudging her frame
over cars and homes

cloud-breathing centipede

the city
as creature
on a conquering path

Standing Over the Great Serpent Mound, 2017

I breathe deep, and in the
distance, hear the chug-pop
of a John Deere,
tall and green like corn stalks,
and the walks
of bumpkin lovers through the fields,

hand-in-hand,
lip-on-lip,
thigh-to-thigh.
They say, "I never want to leave this moment"—
twisting and rolling in dirt, fused
in roots, twined in grass.

I smell the oil on the mechanic's cheek,
crackle-rising smoke in the coal-lit factories—
taste brow-sweat the artist leaks down her
face, and feel her lonesome stomach burble, as eyes
focus on work and only that.
The air is communal,
transcendent; time
is torn and space is singular—each of one
body,
everybody carving a great serpent—
curving through unknowns,
absorbing mysteries by mouthfuls—
in their own eyes, on their own land, soft like blocked lard.

Placement

In Cincinnati,
　　　　the wind and the water
collaborate to set a ghost ship
　　　　　　within the mangled thicket
that hugs the Ohio River
　　　　so that the young, who think
　　　　　　they know everything,
realize the world is much bigger than
　　　　　　　　themselves.

To disrupt the universe,
　　　　I place a cement statue of an owl
　　　　　　deep within the shadows
of a Northeastern Ohio wood.
　　　　　　Like giving a son
a ball, bat, and mitt for the first time,
two lovers happen upon it
　　　　long after I've died—
　　　　　　caped and galvanized in
　　　　moss, engulfed in honeysuckle—
and try to understand
　　　　what it could possibly mean.

As a young man,
I glance at the Standing Rock stones,
　　　　which stack twenty feet high like
used paperbacks, stare me down
　　　　like a falling anvil,
　　　　and cut through the Cuyahoga like
a laser beam, and think of the
　　　　　　Great Spirit,
who whispers to me, "this was not an
　　　　　　accident."

The Sounds of Ash

The wind carries
        whispers, words unsaid,
    and now I know
           it rasps from
     my father's voice. We let him go
from a monolith, on the slope of a

          world, with
       a city like a bonfire—an ember nucleus
    nestled in twigs and logs and leaves—
            below.

       The sound dins
           from the grains of
        desert salt, the crumbles
    of beach sand, the cigarette ash
     of blaze-charred refuse—

and anything else
             that glides

                 adrift.

     All the time spent with smoke in our mouths,
knowing singe would bring him back, transform his matter—he,
emerging
        from the landfill heaps,
     muddling himself
       home, muscle-spasmed, stretching
    out, folding forward—ringing the doorbell
         with his chin, falling back into
       our arms.

The wind carries secrets.

My father died a poor catholic
that hid his faith from
an atheist son like
a mutation.
Now I've captured him in a vial that hangs
around my neck, sealed off
from air, silencing his cries—as a god
could do, as a father's hand does to the back of
the neck of a stifled
tantrum.

Flung

And I remember the days
when my father had flung   me
                          through the air—oil painting
the summer sun,   white core,
                    persimmon slice,   that casts
the shadow of me,   flying,
          soaring like a robber's bag of getaway gold,
      above the swimming pool,   frozen, icy
in time.   Later, I crash back,
                                    jet-up a dash of water
to atmosphere — empyrean   — but not in that image.   no.

There, in that memory, forever, Father and I are smiling
          at each other,   twins.   Me hoping
I never come down, and
                he hoping I don't slip
                          through his grasps.

Additional Acknowledgments

I am incredibly grateful for my mother, grandmother, and sister for their support, as well as my full extended family.

I am very grateful for the many gracious awards and scholarships that were granted to me during the writing of this book. I acknowledge the following families and foundations for their support: the Hare family, the Demen family, the Philippine Kerwer Fund, The Gary L. Green Scholarship, and the Rowland family.

Many thanks to the YSU English Department faculty and staff for their constant support: Steve Reese, Rebecca Barnhouse, Laura Beadling, Stacy Graber, Angela Messenger, Kristine Blair, April Vosch, and others.

Also, an infinite amount of thanks to my friends, who helped make this work possible: N.P. Stokes, McKayla Rockwell, Mallory Rader, Anthony Carbone, Hanna Sassya, Tom Franken, Chris Lattera, Allison Pitinii Davis, Rochelle Hurt, and many more.

Dom **Fonce** is a 24-year-old poet and the Editor-in-Chief of *Volney Road Review*. His work has appeared in *3Elements Review, West Texas Literary Review, the Tishman Review, Obra/Artifact, America's Best Emerging Poets, Black Rabbit Quarterly, Italian Americana, Junto Magazine,* and elsewhere. He lives and writes in Youngstown, Ohio and is a graduate of Youngstown State University.

www.ingramcontent.com/pod-product-compliance
Lightning Source LLC
LaVergne TN
LVHW051610080426
835510LV00020B/3230